Also by Edgar Wollstone

Chronicles of Spy Ladies
Miss Fatale - Greatest World War II Female Spy, In a Fly :
Virginia Hall's Finger Prints over Allies' World War II Victory
Agent Sonya - The Lady of Espionage : Astounding Story of The
Spy Ursula Kuczynski

Life & Legacy In a Fly
Churchill's Better Half - Clementine Churchill : Life and
Legacy of Winston Churchill's Wife, Clementine Churchill, in
a Fly

Sniper Chronicles
Simo Hayha - The Deadliest Sniper In Military History : War
Story of The Deadliest Sniper In Military History, In a Fly
Lady Death - The Beauty With a Sniper : Fascinating Tale of
Lyudmila Pavlichenko, The Deadliest Female Sniper in History
Carlos Hathcock - Vietnam's Most Wanted Sniper : The Sniper's
Extraordinary Engagements During Vietnam War, in a Fly

Operation Mincemeat : A WWII British Deception Operation
Laconia Incident - A High-Risk Military Rescue Operation of
WWII Under The Line of Fire
Operation Vengeance - Killing Admiral Yamamoto : The
Stunning Top Secret WWII Military Operation, In a Fly

Standalone

Maya Angelou's Life In a Fly : Retrospective Voyage Through
the Life of Maya Angelou

Yoshie Shiratori, The Grand Jailbreaker : Heart-Touching Story
of a Japanese Jailbreak Expert

Dawn After Twilight : Industrial Rising of Japan After WW2

Ben L Salomon, The Lone Machine Gunner : A Valiant Story
from WW2, in a Fly

Manoeuvres, Shots and Drops - Dive Bomber Pilot Richard
Halsey Best In World War 2

Hitler's Girls : Captivate Spy Stories of WWII Female Nazi
Spies

Oppenheimer - The Atomic Intelligence : Inside The Brilliant
Mind of Robert Oppenheimer, Father of The Atomic Bomb

Puerto Rican Rambo - Story of Jorge Otero Barreto, The Most
Decorated U.S. Soldier Of The Vietnam War : Sergeant Rock,
In a Fly

Pull It Like Chesty : Life and Legacy of America's Most
Decorated Marine, Chesty Puller

The Dark Encounters in Vietnam : Spine-Chilling Horror
Stories From Vietnam War

The Other Side of Agent Zigzag : Greatest Double Agent of
World War II, Eddie Chapman, In a Fly

The Real Peaky Blinders : Gangster Story of The Actual Peaky Blinders, From Origin to Fall

Niihau Incident : When a Japanese Pilot After Pearl Harbor Attack Crash-Landed on a Hawaiian Island

The Bermuda Triangle of Transylvania, - Hoia Forest -

The Forgotten War Heroes of Vietnam War - Volume II : War Stories of William Pitsenbarger, William Maud Bryant & Jimmie E. Howard

The Forgotten War Heroes of Vietnam War - Volume I : War Stories of George "Bud" Day, Drew Dix, & Jay Vargas

WW2 in Meth - Battling Hallucinations, Enemy Soldiers and Dangers, All Alone, Unarmed and Without Supplies in a Deep Forest

THE OTHER SIDE OF AGENT ZIGZAG

THE OTHER SIDE OF AGENT ZIGZAG

Greatest Double Agent of World War II, Eddie Chapman, In a Fly

Author: Edgar Wollstone

Disclaimer

The content of this book is purely based on the facts learned through various sources. The author and publisher doesn't hold any responsibility based on accuracy, validity, and reliability for the given content. This content is based on the writer's perspective and imagination and doesn't mean to criticize anyone on a personal level. The author and publisher have strived their best to bring forth this amusing content for a wonderful reading experience.

Dedication

At the Feet of Lord

Acknowledgments

Sincerely thankful to everyone for their wholehearted support in making this book a reality.

Book Contents

THE UNBELIEVABLE EDDIE CHAPMAN

Eddie Arnold Chapman

On November 16, 1914, Edward or also called Eddie Arnold Chapman was born in Berwick upon Tweed, England. He was the oldest of three kids. His childhood days were during the Great Depression period. At age 14, he dropped out of school to support his family financially. In the town of Roker, his father managed a tiny bar called the Clipper ship. The business struggled because the elder Chapman was more likely to drink than work. Before moving to London at the age of 17 and enlisting in the Cold stream Guards, where his responsibilities included patrolling the Tower of London, he tried several jobs and experienced a spell of unemployment. Although Chapman appreciated the privileges of the uniform, he quickly grew tired of his responsibilities. He went away with a girl he met in Soho after serving nine months in the army and being given six days of leave. After two months, he was apprehended by the army, who then imprisoned him for 84 days in the military prison of Glasshouse at Aldershot. Chapman was dishonourably discharged from the service after being released.

With his lifestyle outstripping his income due to gambling debts and a liking for fine alcohol, Chapman soon found himself out of money after returning to Soho and working a few temporary jobs, including bartender and film extra. With the money he acquired through his ability as a burglar, he was able to live the life of a wealthy playboy in Soho, where he associated with people like Noel Coward, Ivor Novello, and Marlene Dietrich. After repeated run-ins with the law, he eventually received his first civilian prison sentence, two months in Wormwood Scrubs for forging a check after slipping into criminality, fraud, and petty theft.

He accepted every job that was offered, frequently working as a bartender, extra in movies, dancer, wrestler, and anything else that would keep his access to alcohol and women. He spent much of his free time at Smokey Joe's pub, where he encountered all kinds of criminals and quickly developed a gravitational pull toward the underworld of crime. Chapman started his second job in the 1930s by breaking into houses, taking any things he could find, and forging checks. He received minor penalties for his offences and spent two months in jail for check theft and fraud. Shortly after being released from jail, he was taken into custody again for trespassing and imprisoned for an additional three months.

THE JELLY GANG

Eddie Chapman headed the Jelly Gang, a group of safecrackers, before the war. When the Germans invaded the Island, Chapman was still detained. When he was freed from prison in October 1941, he immediately joined a group that included several people he had met while doing time in Jersey Prison.

He joined West End gangs in London and started safe-cracking. He was imprisoned for these offences for extended periods of time. The gangs broke into safes using gelignite, earning Chapman and his associates the moniker Jelly Gang. James Wells Hunt, whom Chapman met while serving time in prison, assisted Chapman in one of his Jelly Gang crimes. The Jelly Gang then committed a series of high-end store robberies in London, most notably at Isobel's, a furrier, where they took several minks and capes worth a total of 200 pounds.

The group then broke into a pawnbroker, where they stole 15,000 pounds by blowing open four safes. Chapman was so proud of his craftsmanship that he saved newspaper clippings of his robberies in a scrapbook. In order to carry out the crime, Chapman pretended to be a member of the Metropolitan Water Board in order to gain entry to a home in Edgware Road, from which he broke through the wall of the shop next door. The safe's door was then removed using gelignite after it was taken to Hunt's Garage at 39 St. Luke's Mews by him. Eddie made a daring escape shortly after his stint with the Jellies that was reminiscent of actor Errol Flynn in the roles of Captain Blood and Robin Hood.

Chapman was detained in Scotland and accused of blowing up the safe at the Edinburgh Cooperative Society's administrative building. He was released on bail and escaped to Jersey in the Channel Islands, where he tried in vain to resume his criminal activities. Before being taken into custody, Chapman was dining with his future wife-to-be Betty Farmer at the Hotel de la Plage. When he saw plain-clothes officers approaching to take him into custody for crimes committed on the mainland, he made a spectacular getaway through the dining room window, which was closed at the time. Later that night, he committed a sloppy burglary for which he was sentenced to two years in jail in Jersey. Ironically, this avoided him at least 14 additional years in prison on the mainland.

The Jelly Gang fled to Scotland in 1939 as the authorities closed in on them, but their luck eventually ran out there. Chapman and four others were apprehended while attempting to loot the Edinburgh Cooperative Society's offices by a passing police officer who heard a disturbance and looked into it. The four men, however, escaped and ran away to Jersey in the Channel Islands before they could be tried. In spite of the German invasion and occupation of the Channel Islands in July 1940, he was nonetheless imprisoned until his release in October 1941.

He had a pattern of lying about his occupation and the reasons he was at questionable locations at suspicious times. He was also a conman, an extortionist who targeted victims with revealing images as a form of blackmail, and he even threatened to inform an 18-year-old woman's parents that he had infected their daughter with an STD. In essence, Chapman was a horrible person with an extraordinary knack for exploiting others. He lived the high life of a bachelor in London with well-known stars like Marlene Dietrich, who subsequently worked for the OSS, Noel Coward, and Ivor Novello when he wasn't stealing, conspiring, or organising his next task. He later recalled mixing with a variety of challenging characters, including robbers, prostitutes, and flotsam from a great city's nightlife. Chapman was an asset to any intelligence service because he was a natural criminal with the endurance, persistence, talent, and patience needed to succeed. He experimented with gambling and small-time crime there and got into a few scrapes with the cops. Following a succession of robberies for which he was wanted throughout Great Britain in 1939, Edward Arnold Chapman fled to Jersey, a Channel Island just a few miles off the coast of France. There, he had hoped to hide from authorities and possibly continue his illicit activities. They gained quite a notoriety for their extensive use of gelatine explosives placed on the hinges of vault doors to blow them wide open in order to collect the pricey banknotes and jewellery inside, as well as for initially employing their patience to decipher complex safe combinations. The national newspapers were reporting on Chapman's gang's activities. After the group was cornered by investigators but again managed to avoid capture, they were shortly mentioned in the Jersey newspaper. On July 6, 1939, Chapman managed a brief escape from Jersey Prison before being apprehended. His sentence was extended by a year on September 6, 1939. Three months of solitary imprisonment were first, which Chapman resisted by attempting to flee. He received a second three-month sentence in solitary prison for this, which he resisted by ostensibly going on a hunger strike.

After being the target of a massive manhunt across Jersey's marshes, Chapman was finally apprehended by police while he was staying at the Hotel de la Plage. Betty Farmer, Chapman's girlfriend, accompanied him to Jersey. Eddie was imprisoned in Jersey and had no way to leave. But as luck would have it, he soon experienced a change in his life that would last a lifetime. By June 1940, the German war machine had conquered most of Europe while Chapman remained secure in prison. Hitler had complete control over Luxembourg, the Netherlands, France, and Belgium. The Luftwaffe started attacking the remote regions in advance of the predicted invasion of Great Britain, including the Channel Islands, which ended up being the only British Isles sovereign territory actually occupied by the Germans throughout the war. The detainees were now under German control when German troops quickly overran Jersey.

Chapman made friends with 22-year-old Anthony Faramus while he was imprisoned, and the two kept track of each other's locations until the war's end. When Chapman was freed from prison on October 15, 1941, his fortunes altered. A few months before, his friend Faramus had been emancipated, and both men had enjoyed their newfound freedom. Together, they established a tiny barbershop that mostly served German officers and military men. They also became acquaintances with Douglas Stirling, a British national who dealt in the underworld and sold any illegal things he could locate. Together, they started a clandestine business, earning a comfortable living by convincing people to buy their looted goods.

A SPY TO THE GERMANS

Chapman searched for a means to leave the occupied Channel Islands for Britain because life there was hard. They were moved to Fort de Romainville in Paris after writing a letter in German to escape the island. He offered to work as a spy for the Germans, and the Abwehr, the German secret service, eventually accepted him. The Abwehr was in a desperate situation since its network of spies in Britain could only provide it with very poor-quality intelligence. In truth, MI5 had previously apprehended nearly all of the German spies in the UK and hired a number of them as double agents, even though the Abwehr was not aware of this.

Money and time spent in prison are common rewards for a life of crime. On Jersey Island, one of the Channel Islands, Chapman was detained in 1939. Police spotted him breaking and entering a nightclub, and because he was on their "wanted" list, he was unable to escape and was instead put in handcuffs. Years were added to his sentence as he wasted away in his cell after a failed prison break. The German assault on the islands was just luck and coincidence. Like all great crooks, Chapman took the chance to help the Germans in exchange for a reduced sentence and offered his expertise and services. He was able to explain his origins to the Germans and persuade them that he had animosity toward the British.

Chapman received spying training at Le Bourget in France. He collaborated with a number of other Germans at this time. He was provided with enormous sums of cash, fine food, and limitless booze from the Black Market, and lodging in a chateau.

When Chapman assumed he was no longer under German surveillance, a fortuitous accident drastically altered his life. He and a German driver were involved in a bicycle accident one day. The bike and car collided because Chapman was riding on the wrong side of the road. The Germans questioned Chapman and advised him not to cause any more trouble afterward. Chapman, Faramus, and Stirling made the decision to send a letter to the German authorities in the Channel Islands volunteering to work as spies for the Third Reich out of concern for their long-term safety. If he could work a bluff with the Germans, he could undoubtedly be sent across to Britain, Chapman wrote in a letter after deciding to serve with the Germans. Even then, it might have been mere chatter, and he's not going to lie and say there weren't ulterior objectives driving the schemes he started mulling over in his head. He also didn't have them in mind at the same time or in the same mood. The two were transferred to the Fort de Romainville jail, which is located outside of Paris. Chapman was eventually questioned about his prior illegal actions by prison staff members. Dr. Stephan Graumann, also known as von Groning, was one of these men. Despite being on opposing sides of the battle, Chapman and Graumann eventually grew close personal friends. Graumann offered Eddie an offer he couldn't refuse during these sessions. Eddie would be sent back to Britain by German intelligence to carry out certain covert missions that he would later learn about in exchange for his freedom and a substantial payment. Chapman offered to work as a spy for the Germans because he saw an opportunity to escape prison and go back to Great Britain. He accepted the offer out of pure vanity because it was a once-in-a-lifetime opportunity.

General Otto von Stulpnagel, the head of the German soldiers stationed in the Channel Islands, received a letter from Chapman and Faramus offering their services. Additionally, Chapman had a brief encounter with a German officer who after hearing his account promised to contact him later. False accusations that Chapman and Faramus had cut telephone cables in the Channel Islands led to their arrests. They were placed on a train destined for Paris, where their future was uncertain.

Chapman was transported to his new training site, the Villa de la Bretoniere in Nantes, France, while Faramus remained in custody and ultimately ended up in a concentration camp but survived the war. The villa had opulent living quarters. He received a crash school in the finer points of espionage, focusing on hand-to-hand combat, wireless operations, and the use of covert ink. He received training in explosives, radio communications, parachute jumping, and other topics in France at La Bretonnière-la-Claye, Saint-Julien-des-Landes, close to Nantes, under the guidance of Captain Stephan von Gröning, head of the Abwehr in Nantes, before being sent to Britain to carry out acts of sabotage.

Lieutenant Walter Praetorius, also known as Thomas, and Karl Barton, also known as Herman Wojch, oversaw his instruction, which lasted for around three months. Soon, Chapman had mastered a variety of covert arts and was prepared to advance for his new German instructors.

The Germans had been planning to send an undercover agent to Britain for months. When they discovered Chapman, they thought their deepest hopes had been fulfilled. They assigned their new recruit his own V-6523 number and Fritzchen code (Little Fritz). He was now prepared to start his first task. Eddie parachuted from a plane above Cambridge, England, on the night of December 16, 1942, with a radio transmitter, a revolver, a bottle of invisible ink, and a cyanide pill. Unknown to him or the Germans, the British had deciphered the Germans' top-secret codes and knew in advance when an agent Fritzchen, or little Fritz, as Chapman was known to the Germans, would be sent into the United Kingdom. He discovered that he had been given a sizable sum of money with the German stamp clearly visible and wrapped around the bills when he landed and went through his belongings. Chapman gave his interrogators all the details regarding his time in occupied France and the mission the Germans had assigned him since he was more than prepared to comply. He even offered to fight the Germans on behalf of the British.

The British were well aware of his ambitions to infiltrate Britain, but they were still unsure of his precise identity, which was unknown to Abwehr and Eddie Chapman. By using their Ultra decryptions of German radio communications, the British were able to read German cables and keep tabs on German spies as they approached English beaches. The British were able to capture and turn German spies who went on to work against their former employers under the threat of death by using their Twenty Committee or Double Cross Organization. To protect themselves, the majority of these spies worked with the British. After arriving, Chapman surrendered himself to the local police, who contacted the Secret Intelligence Service. Chapman shared with them his experience being approached by the Abwehr and his offer to work for the British in its place. German intelligence officers and couriers frequently met in neutral Portugal in March 1943 because of Chapman's passion and dedication, which impressed the Germans. He entered Lisbon using fake documents using the name Hugh Anson while sailing on a British merchant ship. When Chapman met his Abwehr handlers, they gave him an explosive device that looked like a chunk of "coal" that he was to carry onto the ship and plant in a coal bunker.

Instead, Chapman found the bomb and gave it to the captain of the ship with the directive to give it over to the War Office. He and his Abwehr handlers relocated to a safe house in Nazi-occupied Norway from Lisbon, and there, in a covert ceremony held in Oslo, he received the Iron Cross, Germany's highest accolade. The medal has only ever been given to one British person, Chapman. Chapman directly lied about his target evaluations to make sure the bombs went beyond the city's perimeter, giving the Germans false information about his findings and saving the lives of thousands of Londoners as a result

Chapman was a prime target for the men of MI-5 to turn on. He was wanted for a number of crimes that occurred on British soil, and they now had him in their sights. He had two options: serve a significant period of time in prison or cooperate with the British by providing the Abwehr with fake information. Chapman chose the first option and made the decision to collaborate with his countrymen. He offered to work as a spy for the Germans, and the Abwehr, the German secret service, eventually accepted him. The Abwehr was in a desperate situation since its network of spies in Britain could only provide it with very poor-quality intelligence. In truth, MI5 had previously apprehended nearly all of the German spies in the UK and hired a number of them as double agents, even though the Abwehr was not aware of this.

FROM THE DOUBLE-CROSS TO THE IRON CROSS

Chapman was dispatched to Camp 020, a covert facility where all arrested German operatives were housed. The location, a huge, sprawling house close to Ham Common in West London, was known by its formal name, Latch mere House. Eddie would learn the nuances of British tradecraft here before being assigned to future tasks. Chapman admitted to his interrogators that the main task assigned to him by the Abwehr was to obliterate the De Havilland airplane manufacturing facility, which produced the quick-moving Mosquito aircraft. The Mosquito had incredible speed and manoeuvrability because it was built of wood. It was his responsibility to detonate the facility in Hatfield, Hertfordshire.

The British gave Chapman permission to claim that he had destroyed the Mosquito facility with a little assistance from a magician by the name of Jasper Maskelyne. Maskelyne was descended from a magically gifted family. By hiding the Suez Canal and misleading the enemy at the Battle of El Alamein, Maskelyne assisted the British in tricking the Germans during the war.

Chapman was viewed by the Abwehr as the perfect spy. Because he was still wanted by the police for his crimes committed on the UK mainland, he claimed to be hostile to the British state. He might be able to recruit more spies for the Germans thanks to his ties in the criminal underground, and his knowledge of explosives would allow him to carry out sabotage operations.

The Germans specifically wanted him to strike the Hertfordshire-based De Havilland aircraft factory, which produced the dreaded Mosquito bomber. Maskelyne collaborated closely with a number of British military units, including the camouflage division of the Air Ministry, to fabricate a series of explosions that would appear to German observation aircraft that flew overhead that the De Havilland plant had been destroyed. For the Mosquito plant, Maskelyne and his crew erected phoney tarpaulins to project the impression of total destruction.

Chapman did his part by utilising his predetermined code to wirelessly notify the Abwehr that everything had gone according to plan. "FFFFF WALTER BLOWN IN TWO PLACES," he wrote. Graumann sent his favourite spy a congratulatory message as soon as he received the good news. The British coordinated the publication of a bogus news story about the "destruction" of the De Havilland factory in the London Daily Express edition of February 1, 1943, in order to thoroughly confuse the Germans. Graumann received the newspaper in Lisbon and read with curiosity how his master spy had fared. Eddie Chapman received the Iron Cross from the German government in recognition of his outstanding work.

THE OPERATION DAMP SQUIB AND PORTUGAL

Eddie Chapman's name wasn't initially as widely known among World War II espionage students as other spies like Juan Pujol Garcia alias Garbo, Richard Sorge, and Elyesa Bazna aka Cicero. All of that changed, though, when MI-5, the British Intelligence Service, at long last declassified 1,800 documents about Eddie Chapman's work as a double agent during World War II and gave them to the British National Archives. Additionally, some of these records were added to the U.S. National Archives in College Park, Maryland, and are now accessible to the general public. What these documents show is a severely broken man who was a womaniser and had extramarital encounters while also having a child outside of marriage. They describe a guy who was entertained by two competing intelligence services, the British Intelligence Service, which also utilised Chapman for its own purposes, and the German Abwehr, led by Admiral Wilhelm Canaris. The Abwehr, on the other hand, parachuted Chapman into Great Britain on an intelligence operation while carrying a bundle of clearly marked German marks. On the British side, they attended Chapman's every whim while sending two plainclothes police officers to live with him around the clock.

Chapman also took part in a different successful trick against the Abwehr. As part of Operation Squid, false information on the squid trials of a top-secret British anti-submarine weapon was sent to the Abwehr. Radio messages from the Abwehr discussing the scheme were deciphered by code breakers from Intelligence

Services Knox (ISK) at Bletchley Park. Lieutenant Commander Ewen Montagu of the Double Cross Committee wrote a bogus letter on September 4, 1944, and gave Chapman instructions to smuggle it into the Abwehr.

MI5 was eagerly waiting for the return of Chapman, unlike the Germans, in the hopes that he would gather crucial intelligence about the adversary as a reliable asset. He was tasked with recalling a set of inquiries that the Allies sought responses to. The document was cleverly crafted to prevent its contents from revealing to German espionage any gaps in the Allied knowledge should Chapman be compromised. It was determined that for Chapman to reach Lisbon, he would accompany the squad of a commercial ship and abandon the ship once it berthed in Portugal. Prior to Chapman embarking on his journey aboard The City of Lancaster, a ship sailing from Liverpool, a false identity, Hugh Anson, was created and the necessary papers were obtained. He recommended trying to blow the ship with a device posed as a piece of coal to be deposited in the coal bunker after speaking with Germans at their mission in Lisbon. In answer to a reaction to examples of German explosive devices from the British anti-wreckage unit, he did this.

He received two explosives, but he gave the pair to the ship's captain instead. The British conducted a noticeable inquiry when the ship arrived back in Britain, making sure rumours would reach the Germans. This prevented the Germans from questioning Chapman's commitment and prevented them from seeing the ship was undamaged throughout the return voyage. Chapman was ordered to instruct in German spying in Oslo while Norway was under occupation. Chapman was given the

Iron Cross after receiving a debriefing from von Gröning for his role in allegedly causing damage to the de Havilland plant and Lancaster City, which made him the very first Englishman to do so ever since the war between France and Prussia happened in 1870–1871 Nicholas Booth argues that since the only the members of the armed force was awarded Iron Cross, Chapman's Iron Cross may have actually been a second-class War Merit Cross or Kriegsverdienstkreuz. Chapman was commissioned into the Germany Army as either an oberleutnant or first lieutenant.

A few months later, Mr. Chapman exposed a German sabotage scheme in Portugal by informing the captain of a British ship about a coal-shaped bomb he had hidden on board the ship for his German employers. After that, he vanished into occupied Europe. According to Mr. Masterman in an interview with The Daily Mail, reports of a mystery person in Oslo in 1944 who was granted complete control of a private yacht while speaking loudly in awful German and wearing a suit with a pepper-and-salt pattern began to circulate. "Based solely on those details, we assumed it was Zig-Zag.

He dropped again into England in the late summer of 1944, but this time he hit concrete instead of a farm, which caused him to lose all of his teeth. In order to ensure accuracy, he was tasked with reporting to Germany about its rocket attacks on London. However, he exaggerated where the rockets were landing, which led the Germans to reroute bombs into the suburbs.

THE ZIGZAG CASE

At Camp 020, Chapman studied under and was instructed by some of the most significant agents of the British Secret Service. Colonel Robin Tin Eye Stephens, the base's commander, Lord Victor Rothschild, a scientist who assisted Eddie with explosives, and Captain Ronnie Reed, an authority in wireless communications, were among them. However, one British commander had little interest in working with Chapman. Chapman's case officer, as they would say in the spy world, was Major Michael Ryde, and the two of them hit it off right away. Chapman's habit of frequenting London's clubs to look for prostitutes and his intoxication bothered Ryde. Chapman seemed very dissatisfied at the moment; he was expansive, gloomy, and absolutely disreputable, the man claimed. Chapman's babysitter during his stay in England, Thomas Robertson, received a letter from Ryde stating that the Zigzag case must be closed down at the earliest feasible moment. Ryde's superiors quickly altered his perspective.

Chapman had time to court a variety of women, all of whom he cared deeply for when he wasn't working his hidden profession. When he was dispatched to Norway by Graumann, he worked alongside Dagmar Lahlum, a stunning Norwegian who was also a German spy. Later, he admitted to Dagmar that the man was an agent from Britain, however, she kept the information to herself. Freda Stevenson, who had a child with Eddie and was given the name Diane, was another love. Eddie wed Betty Farmer, a woman he dumped behind at the Hotel de la Plage in Jersey years earlier when the war was over.

Chapman complied with the British government's approval when the Abwehr ordered him to return to Germany. After that, he spent some time in Oslo, Norway, at a spy academy where he met Dagmar and picked up boat sailing skills. At one time, Chapman proposed using a bomb to assassinate Adolf Hitler while he was present at a rally. It appears that Dr. Graumann promised to accompany Chapman to a rally for Hitler and secure a front-row seat for him. Winston Churchill, the British prime minister, was informed about the Zigzag case by Duff Cooper, a prominent member of the intelligence community. Cooper claimed that he had a lengthy conversation about Zigzag with the prime minister, who had expressed a keen interest in the situation.

AGENT ZIGZAG

Eddie Chapman

The British Secret Service gave Eddie Chapman the codename Zigzag, which was fitting for a double spy from World War II. He was referred to by the Germans as Fritz or Fritzchen, an endearing diminutive. Eddie Chapman resembled a battered Errol Flynn with his gorgeous, off-kilter face and pencil-thin moustache. He even spent some time working as a movie extra. Eddie engaged in numerous activities.

Eddie Chapman handed himself to the British and became Agent Zigzag after providing his criminal services to the Nazis in exchange for being released from prison. In the early stages of World War II, when U-boats and the Luftwaffe patrolled the

English Channel and British skies, anxious Britons believed that German spies lurked around every corner. Nobody realised that Germany's top spy, who was assigned to trouble Britain and undermine the fight against fascism, wasn't even a committed Nazi. He wasn't even German, in actuality.

After conversing with Chapman, Stephens concluded in a report that Chapman needs to be utilised to the fullest extent possible. He really does intend to help the British fight the Germans. He is perfectly suited to be an agent because of his bravery and ingenuity.

Zigzag was given the covert mission to re-infiltrate the ranks of the Abwehr in order to gather information while disguising himself. Using his wireless radio, he made contact with the Germans and informed them that he was prepared to carry out the sabotage task they had originally assigned to him. The Germans were unaware that Chapman and his MI5 handler were planning to carry out a cunning deception operation to make it appear as though sabotage had occurred. In actuality, it was an excellent ruse to build credibility and confidence with no casualties.

MI5 made the decision to send Chapman undercover once more in order to learn more about the Abwehr. Chapman made radio contact with the Germans while being watched over by an MI5 officer and informed them that he was getting ready to carry out his sabotage mission at the De Havilland factory. He was dispatched to the Hatfield facility with an MI5 minder to devise a strategy so he could later inform his German controllers of what he had done.

One of the most impressive deception schemes of the Second World War was the assault itself. An extensive system of camouflage was set up at the De Havilland facility on the night of January 29 and 30, 1943, to give the impression to German reconnaissance aircraft that a huge bomb had exploded within the business's power plant. Buildings were concealed with tarpaulins and corrugated iron sheets painted to seem from the air as if they were the half-demolished remnants of walls and roofs, and bomb-damaged transformers were made out of wood and papier-mache. The power plant was covered in rubble and debris to give the impression that it had been flung there by an explosion. Separately, MI5 coordinated the placement of a false report about an explosion at a factory outside of London in the Daily Express.

The hoax was so effective that it even fooled the employees of the factory. Chapman radioed the Germans to let them know that the factory's power plant had been successfully "demolished." Chapman's work was praised by Abwehr. In March 1943, he returned to Germany via the neutral nation of Portugal before continuing on to a German-occupied safe house in Norway. To his surprise, he received the Iron Cross, Germany's highest honour, in appreciation for his service to the Abwehr. He was the first and only British citizen to ever get this medal.

Later, British intelligence agent Sir John Master man provided the following account: Mr. Chapman called Scotland Yard after landing in a field close to the Cambridgeshire town of Ely and volunteered his services as a double agent. Due to their ability to decipher German codes, the British were able to predict his arrival and set up his deafening pseudo-explosion at the power plant of aircraft production. The British then placed debris nearby while a roof was sprayed with camouflage paint to resemble blast damage. German reconnaissance images appeared to support Mr. Chapman's efforts. When he later supplied false reports to his masters via British intelligence about troop movements and shipbuilding, they had a little issue doing so.

AGENT ZIGZAG SYSTEMATICALLY UNDERMINES THE NAZIS

Chapman immediately made it clear to his new superiors that they had hit proverbial gold during his time working for MI5. They had one of Germany's best agents, and he was anxious to work with them and thwart the Abwehr's plans in Britain and overseas. He started by convincing them that the de Havilland factory had been destroyed. British spies aired fabricated news reports to further the illusion by making the factory appear to have been completely destroyed. The mission was declared a perfect success on both sides of the English Channel when German reconnaissance planes returned with images of the apparent wreckage.

In order to capitalise on this triumph, Chapman's MI5 handlers planned to have him returned to von Grönig on board The City of Lancaster, a commercial ship sailing to Lisbon, Portugal, which was a neutral country during World War II. Along the way, he got two bombs from his German superiors, purportedly to blow up the ship, but he immediately sent them to MI5 for analysis. Eddie Chapman was so highly regarded by this point that the Abwehr transported him to Norway where was captured by the Nazis and hired him to instruct the coming generation of Nazi spies. But he wouldn't be permitted to remain in one place for an extended period of time.

In June 1944, he was returning to England to report on American military forces, the application of SONAR, and the results of the V-1 and V-2 rockets that had been screeching into the British sky in an effort to cruelly inflict deaths on the Allies. He was unaware that the July 20 assassination attempt had been hatched only a few weeks after he had returned to England, and the Führer promptly dissolved the Abwehr. Without a job, Chapman endured the rest of the war by disseminating false information and purposefully exaggerating the success of the German rocket programme. Chapman received the Iron Cross, Second Class, and 110,000 Reichsmarks as one of Germany's top spies, making him the only British citizen to ever receive the award.

Despite his many accomplishments and incomparable usefulness, MI5 had grown weary of a guy who they finally viewed as a liability. On November 28, 1944, Chapman was sworn to secrecy and expelled from the secret service. Agent Zigzag had disappeared. Returning to a life of crime, Chapman Eddie Chapman had the ideal opportunity to resume his criminal career after being released from MI5.

Chapman served as a double agent for the next four years, a lone British spy at the centre of the German Secret Service who at one point offered to kill Hitler for his countrymen. He travelled throughout Europe using various aliases, concocted schemes, disseminated false information, and, remarkably, managed to maintain his claims when subjected to prolonged interrogation. He even made some money and attracted attractive ladies along the way. Chapman received the Iron Cross from the Nazis, who hailed him as a hero. He became the only wartime agent to receive such a reward after he was pardoned for his crimes in

Britain. Both nations supported his mistress and the mother of his child.

Sixty years after the war's end and 10 years after Chapman's passing, MI5 has finally declassified all of Chapman's records, making more than 1,800 pages of top-secret information available for the first time and enabling the complete Agent Zigzag story to be revealed. Agent Zigzag is a compelling tale of betrayal, love, and allegiance that provides a rare look into the psyche of espionage and its hazy line between loyalty and treachery.

BACK TO LONDON

Graumann informed Chapman in 1944 that he would be returning to England on another intelligence operation. Chapman's new task was to learn as much as he could about Britain's most recent efforts to follow German U-boats because the Abwehr still did not know that he was working for British intelligence. Additionally, if at all feasible, he was to acquire the equipment employed by the Royal Air Force in its new night fighters. German aircraft dropped Chapman over England, close to Cambridge, on June 29, 1944. He met with the local police, much like upon his previous landing, who then contacted London. When Chapman informed his handlers of his new assignment, a sophisticated disinformation effort was started to deceive the Berlin men.

Agent Zigzag was getting agitated and irritated by this point. He intended to return to Paris and carry on his covert efforts there. After much-heated discussion, it was decided that Chapman's double agent status should terminate after MI-5 rejected that proposal. Agent Zigzag received word in November 1944 that the British government no longer required his services. Along with the remaining 1,000 pounds from the funds sent to him by the Abwehr, Eddie left with 6,000 pounds in cash from the British. Graumann assumed that his prize agent had been either killed or taken prisoner when, after several hard months of waiting, he had not heard from Chapman.

AFTER RETIREMENT

When Chapman retired, MI5 voiced some concern that he may turn to crime once his money ran out and that, if he were to be captured, he would ask for mercy due to his highly secret wartime service. He associated with thieves and blackmailers, as was expected, and ran afoul of the law for a number of offences, including smuggling gold across the Mediterranean in 1950. He frequently obtained character references from retired intelligence agents who attested to his significant contribution to the war effort.

Chapman returned to his profession in crime when the war was over. He reconnected with his old friends from earlier years and dabbled in protection ring activities and the black market in London. In October 1954, he and Betty welcomed a daughter they named Suzanne. In addition to carrying gold illegally across the Mediterranean, he purchased stock in the Flamingo, a ship that was used for criminal activity. The family relocated to South Africa in the 1960s.

Chapman attempted to make money by having his wartime memoirs serialised in France, but instead he was charged under the Official Secrets Act and fined £50. When they were scheduled to appear in the News of the World a few years later, the entire issue was pulped. His final assignment was to provide a report on the success of the V-1 buzz bomb attacks on British cities. Chapman provided Germany with misleading information, which made the V-1 and later V-2 rocket assaults less successful.

At this time in history, Britain was regrettably a crook's paradise, with countless chances for fraud, theft, and other shady business dealings. The criminal formerly known as Agent Zigzag also possessed exceptional immunity, as the British government would never risk his exposure to any police officers or newspaper reporters who might persuade him to spill his secrets in the light of his involvement in the most daring espionage operations of the war. Chapman was able to commit more crimes because of the money from Abwehr and the free pass from MI5. Even though the Zigzag case and the Double Cross System were shrouded in secrecy, it wasn't long before the truth came to light. Before attempting to break lines and publish his story in the British newspaper News of the World, Chapman was the first to do it. He did so in France. His attempts were repeatedly thwarted by fines and objections, but in 1953 he finally published his memoirs.

In contrast to his murky job and wartime exploits, the rest of his life was calm. He established a calm life as a businessman and antique dealer in his later years. He subsequently married Betty Farmer, the girlfriend he had abandoned on Jersey island, and they produced a daughter. On December 11, 1977, Edward Chapman, 83, passed away from heart failure. Anthony Faramus subsequently became the butler for Hollywood icon Cary Grant after escaping the hell of the Mauthausen-Gusen concentration camp with only one lung and seven ribs remaining.

In response to the question of whether he missed his previous life of crime, daring, and espionage in 1960, Chapman only said: "I do a bit. I'm regret-free. I have no remorse for anything I've done. I prefer to think of myself as a good bad guy. Now that you are familiar with the wacky reality of Agent Zigzag, find out about the audacious efforts of Juan Pujol Garca, aka Agent Garbo, the independent Spanish spy who provided Britain with Nazi secrets. Then, read about Dusko Popov's escapades, the real-life James Bond who served as an inspiration for Ian Fleming.

In the latter stages of the war, he also provided the Germans with bogus intelligence that prevented buzz bombs from falling on central London. It appeared that patriotism had little to do with any of this. The British and the Germans gave Mr. Chapman gifts in exchange for forgetting about the prison time they had in store for him. In his later years, Mr. Chapman who is left by his wife Betty, a daughter, and four grandchildren found a more subdued calling: he managed a health farm in the 1980s, north of London. German authorities pardoned Mr. Chapman in the same way that the British did. Former German espionage controller for Mr. Chapman, Baron Stefan von Grunen, was delighted to attend the wedding of his daughter.

The Eddie Chapman Story, his book, was eventually released in 1953. The Real Eddie Chapman Story, Eddie's autobiography from 1966, omitted a lot of the juicy details that would later become widely known. Christopher Plummer starred in the Triple Cross film that was based on his life. The autobiography of British citizen Eric Pleasants, who enlisted in the German army and served in the British Free Corps of the Waffen-SS during the war, was ghost written by Chapman. While he was detained in Jersey, Chapman claimed to have crossed paths with Pleasants. Published in 1957 was I Killed to Live: The Story of Eric Pleasants as Told to Eddie Chapman. While residing in Italy in 1967, Chapman started a career as an antiquarian. At the age of 83, in December 1997, Agent Zigzag passed away bringing an original World War II espionage tale to a close.

THE SPY I LOVED

Dagmar Lahlum

Chapman was engaged to two women, each of whom was living in a different conflict zone. When he met Dagmar Lahlum in Norway, he was still committed to Freda Stevenson back in the United Kingdom. Lahlum was being treated by von Gröning, and Stevenson was receiving financial support from MI5. Chapman told Dagmar that he was a British spy while he was in Norway, but thankfully Dagmar was connected to the Norwegian resistance. They collaborated to obtain intelligence on the Germans after she learned that her lover was not a German officer.

After the war, he left both ladies behind and instead wed Betty Farmer, the woman he had hurriedly left at the Hotel de la Plage in 1938. In 1954, he gave birth to a daughter named Suzanne with Farmer. Dagmar served a six-month prison sentence for consorting with an ostensibly German officer: thinking that Chapman was dead, she was unable to show that he was a British agent. In 1994, they briefly reconnected. Chapman passed away before he could clear her name.

Betty Chapman was a remarkable woman in her own right. She is best known as "Mrs. Zigzag," Eddie Chapman's wife, and "Agent Zigzag," the most notorious double agent of the Second World War. 18-year-old Betty Farmer was being courted in 1939 by a man who was not only attractive and charming but also, it would appear, worked in the film business. She was taken aback by the two suspicious-looking men who accompanied them when he took her away for a few days of vacation in Jersey, but she kept her worries to herself. During Sunday lunch on their second day apart, with the sun dancing on the water outside, Betty's lover gave her a quick kiss before throwing himself through a shuttered window and fleeing down the beach while being pursued by the police. He had repeatedly promised that he shall go, but he shall always come back, and Betty had no choice but to trust him.

Eddie Chapman, the most extraordinary double agent of World War II, used this method to court the lady who would eventually become his wife. Ben Macintyre's most recent novel, Agent

Zigzag, tells the incredible story of this man. Eddie also played both sides of the relationship game. With one of his lovers, Freda Stevenson, he had already had a kid, and they kept in touch. He also fell in love with Dagmar Lahlum, a daring young woman who worked for the Norwegian resistance and was posted to Norway by the Nazis. However, a spy who is in love is a spy who may be persuaded. British and German intelligence, respectively, utilised Freda and Dagmar as negotiating chips. Eddie began his career as a thief with the infamous, safe-cracking Jelly Gang. With the money he made from his crimes, he was able to live a lavish social life in Soho's underworld, where Noel Coward and Marlene Dietrich were among his acquaintances. However, by the time Eddie brought Betty to Jersey, he had become wanted by the British authorities and was ultimately detained there.

The concept of having a relationship with, or even being married to, a spy has always been seductive, and this idea has spawned a variety of stories and characters, most notably, of course, James Bond and his ladies. Chapman married Betty after the war, and they remained together until his passing in 1997. But according to Macintyre, Chapman must have been a very terrible spouse. He was constantly looking for new adventures, whether they were romantic or not.

MOVIES AND BOOKS

Although Chapman has long been acknowledged as one of Britain's most accomplished double spies, his complete narrative has only recently come to light thanks to the National Archives opening of its records. After the war, the British government made an effort to conceal Mr. Chapman's double agent activities.

However, a senior War Office official provided him with a character reference in 1948 when he was in front of a British court on a charge involving cash transactions, referring to him as "one of the bravest men who served in the last war.

The references to his activities on behalf of Britain were removed by the authorities when his biography, "The Eddie Chapman Story," was published in 1953 and started to be serialised in British media. However, the War Office later acknowledged that Mr. Chapman's claims of acting as a double agent were accurate.

Chapman retired from the MI5 around the conclusion of the war, and his prison terms were overturned. Because old habits are hard to break, he allegedly smuggled contraband while residing in Algeria in the 1950s.

He wrote "The Eddie Chapman Story" in 1953 and promoted the Christopher Plummer-starring film Triple Cross by making an appearance on the popular national quiz show To Tell The Truth in 1965.

Following the war, a film on Eddie's life was produced in 1966, starring Christopher Plummer. According to the Wikipedia article, Plummer claimed that Chapman was supposed to serve as a technical adviser on the movie in his book.

However, the French government would not let him enter because he was still sought for allegedly plotting to kidnap the Moroccan Sultan. This accusation might be scandalous in some lives, but in Eddie's tale, it hangs around like an unpaid parking fine.

Based on the biography The Real Eddie Chapman Story, which Chapman and Frank Owen co-wrote, was the 1966 film Triple Cross. Terence Young, who had met Chapman before the war, was the film's director. Christopher Plummer portrayed Chapman in the movie. Chapman was dissatisfied in the movie since it only had a shaky connection to reality.

French television (ORTF) created a short film in 1967 that featured a private à la maison interview with Chapman in fluent French. Former mobster and snoop Eddie Chapman is a journalist named Pierre Dumayet. Series: Five columns to a row. Director: JP Gallo. Broadcast at 19:29 on January 6, 1967. Along with Tony Benn, Lord Dacre, James Rusbridger, Miles Copeland, and others, Chapman made a lengthy appearance on the Channel 4 discussion programme After Dark in May 1989.

A Time watch documentary based on Eddie Chapman's book, Double Agent: The Eddie Chapman Story, was aired on BBC Two in 2011 and was hosted by Ben Macintyre. A shortened reading of the book was televised in 2012. A movie about Chapman with stars Stanley Baker or Michael Rennie was supposed to be made in the 1950s, but it was never made.

In conclusion, The Eddie Chapman Story (1953), Free Agent: The Further Adventures of Eddie Chapman (1955), and The Real Eddie Chapman Story (1956) are three novels that chronicle Chapman's wartime survival after he returned to Britain in June 1944. (1966). Zigzag - The amazing Wartime Exploits of Double Agent Eddie Chapman by Nicholas Booth and Agent Zigzag: The True Wartime Story of Eddie Chapman, Lover, Betrayer, Hero, Spy by Ben Macintyre both tell Eddie Chapman's story.

CONCLUSION

Eddie Chapman is evidence that a superhero need not be a face-masher with bulging muscles. He wasn't a huge man, he wasn't a murderer, and he avoided conflict whenever he could. He nevertheless succeeded in becoming one of the most colourful war heroes in British history by playing both the British and the Germans off one another, engaging in a variety of escapades, crossing a variety of redlines, and generally living up to expectations for a professional spy. Chapman liked himself, adventure, and his nation, presumably in that order, according to one of his former bosses.

Eddie Chapman was a charismatic con artist, philanderer, and crook. Additionally, he was among the most outstanding double spies that Britain has ever produced. The villain was a hero, and the traitor was a man of loyalty. Chapman's difficulty in determining where one character ended and the other began was shared by his girlfriends, spymasters, and spying employers. Chapman was parachuted into Britain in 1941 with a handgun, a wireless, and a cyanide tablet on his person with orders from the Abwehr to blow up an airplane manufacturing after receiving spy training in German-occupied France. He instead got in touch with the British Secret Service, MI5.

Eddie is categorically unsuited for life in the real world. He was an outlaw, a minor bad guy, a con man, a forger, and a safe cracker. When the Nazis conquered the Channel Islands in 1940, he was imprisoned in Jersey and gave himself to the Germans as a spy in order to escape. He was trained in France before being dropped into England, where he immediately turned himself in, swore allegiance to that country, and offered his services as a double agent.

But at the same time, he was reckless and unreliable before the war, and he had never encountered a law he could follow. Agent ZigZag during the war was magnificent, brave, loyal, and sincere. In order to thwart his German handlers' plans and provide false information to them, he performed things that an ordinary person would never have done. He also did this while cheerfully and charmingly overcoming danger and devastation.

He was a straight-backed hero when the war ended, but he soon returned to a life of frivolity and squalor.

Review Request

Eternally grateful for your recent purchase. We hope you love it! If you do, would you consider posting an online review? This helps us to continue providing great efforts and coherent growth.

Thank you in advance for your review and for being a preferred customer.

THE END

Don't miss out!

Visit the website below and you can sign up to receive emails whenever Edgar Wollstone publishes a new book. There's no charge and no obligation.

https://books2read.com/r/B-A-CXBO-MAGLC

BOOKS 2 READ

Connecting independent readers to independent writers.

Did you love *The Other Side of Agent Zigzag : Greatest Double Agent of World War II, Eddie Chapman, In a Fly*? Then you should read *Carlos Hathcock - Vietnam's Most Wanted Sniper : The Sniper's Extraordinary Engagements During Vietnam War, in a Fly*[1] by Edgar Wollstone!

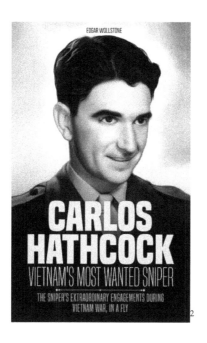

Carlos Hathcock, the man known to many in the US as the **deadliest American sniper**, indomitable and fearsome, an indispensable asset during the **Vietnam War**, is a soft-spoken and gentle family man to his folks. The man dressed in the green marine uniform flaunted a white feather on his hat, a sheer badassery, making open ribaldry of the enemy forces and daring

1. https://books2read.com/u/mvNEqj

2. https://books2read.com/u/mvNEqj

them to spot him amidst the green patina of rice fields in Southern Vietnam. This habit of Carlos had earned him the moniker "**White Feather**". As was common during war, the enemy had placed a few thousand dollars bounty on many US **snipers**. But Carlos' notoriety and badassery was so famed and feared among the enemies that they placed a whopping 30,000-dollar bounty on his head. With 93 confirmed kills and over 300 unconfirmed, Carlos had sealed his place among the world's deadliest snipers. Crawling his way to the den of his target, waiting in the prowl embracing the stillness of the dead, pulling his trigger with immaculate precision, and returning his way to his tent on the hilltop undetected, with such finesse and expertise that Carlos makes it all look effortless. But knowing the nuanced details of his painfully sluggish mode of transport that would take at least days before he "worms" his way through the swampy and muddy rice fields, during day and night, one cannot stop to think what a harrowing experience it would have been. Carlos, himself was homesick and lonely but that didn't dent his resolve to butcher the men who had no qualms in firing away at his fellow marines. The lonely nights that Carlos spends ruminating on his bunker on the hilltop, listening to the wind howling through every chink on the makeshift roof, he was reminded of his grandma's cottage in the countryside in Arkansas. How lovely and boisterous had those days been, Carlos was nostalgic, and his heart had doddered off to a place of remove. It happens often, on nights like these. This is a riveting tale of an US marine who was enamored by his profession, lived, and died completely surrendering to the sport of sniping. His tale of scaling great heights and eventually losing it all is equally inspiring and heart breaking.

Also by Edgar Wollstone

Chronicles of Spy Ladies

Miss Fatale - Greatest World War II Female Spy, In a Fly :
Virginia Hall's Finger Prints over Allies' World War II Victory
Agent Sonya - The Lady of Espionage : Astounding Story of The
Spy Ursula Kuczynski

Life & Legacy In a Fly

Churchill's Better Half - Clementine Churchill : Life and
Legacy of Winston Churchill's Wife, Clementine Churchill, in
a Fly

Sniper Chronicles

Simo Hayha - The Deadliest Sniper In Military History : War
Story of The Deadliest Sniper In Military History, In a Fly
Lady Death - The Beauty With a Sniper : Fascinating Tale of
Lyudmila Pavlichenko, The Deadliest Female Sniper in History
Carlos Hathcock - Vietnam's Most Wanted Sniper : The Sniper's
Extraordinary Engagements During Vietnam War, in a Fly

Killing Silently : American Sniper Chris Kyle's Lethal Moments
Sniper of Vietnam War : The Shots of Marine Sniper Chuck
Mawhinney, In a Fly
500+ Kills - Sniper Ivan Sidorenko : WWII Hero of the Soviet
Union
Deadly Sniper Duels - The War Story of Controversial Duel
Between The Soviet Sniper Expert Vasily Zaitsev And The
Mysterious Top Nazi Sniper in WW2

Titan Fails
Titan Fails - Vietnam War : How & Why America Lost the
Vietnam War

War Classics In a Fly
Battle of the Atlantic, in a Fly : Long 2,075 days of War in
World War 2
Battle of Midway, WWII Naval Battle in a Fly : Captivating
Read on the Motives, Strategies, Tactics and the Winning
Events of the Decisive World War II Battle
Battle of Okinawa, in a Fly : A Chilling Epitome on the
Bloodiest Battle in Pacific Theater of World War 2
D-DAY, in A Fly : Deceptive Operation Bodyguard, Gruesome
Battle of Normandy and the Aftermath
American Civil War, in a Fly

World War II Military Operations

Operation Mincemeat : A WWII British Deception Operation
Laconia Incident - A High-Risk Military Rescue Operation of WWII Under The Line of Fire
Operation Vengeance - Killing Admiral Yamamoto : The Stunning Top Secret WWII Military Operation, In a Fly

Standalone

Maya Angelou's Life In a Fly : Retrospective Voyage Through the Life of Maya Angelou

Yoshie Shiratori, The Grand Jailbreaker : Heart-Touching Story of a Japanese Jailbreak Expert

Dawn After Twilight : Industrial Rising of Japan After WW2

Ben L Salomon, The Lone Machine Gunner : A Valiant Story from WW2, in a Fly

Manoeuvres, Shots and Drops - Dive Bomber Pilot Richard Halsey Best In World War 2

Hitler's Girls : Captivate Spy Stories of WWII Female Nazi Spies

Oppenheimer - The Atomic Intelligence : Inside The Brilliant Mind of Robert Oppenheimer, Father of The Atomic Bomb

Puerto Rican Rambo - Story of Jorge Otero Barreto, The Most Decorated U.S. Soldier Of The Vietnam War : Sergeant Rock, In a Fly

Pull It Like Chesty : Life and Legacy of America's Most Decorated Marine, Chesty Puller

The Dark Encounters in Vietnam : Spine-Chilling Horror Stories From Vietnam War

The Other Side of Agent Zigzag : Greatest Double Agent of World War II, Eddie Chapman, In a Fly

The Real Peaky Blinders : Gangster Story of The Actual Peaky Blinders, From Origin to Fall

Niihau Incident : When a Japanese Pilot After Pearl Harbor Attack Crash-Landed on a Hawaiian Island

The Bermuda Triangle of Transylvania, - Hoia Forest -

The Forgotten War Heroes of Vietnam War - Volume II : War Stories of William Pitsenbarger, William Maud Bryant & Jimmie E. Howard

The Forgotten War Heroes of Vietnam War - Volume I : War Stories of George "Bud" Day, Drew Dix, & Jay Vargas

WW2 in Meth - Battling Hallucinations, Enemy Soldiers and Dangers, All Alone, Unarmed and Without Supplies in a Deep Forest

Ingram Content Group UK Ltd.
Milton Keynes UK
UKHW020635170723
425272UK00014B/311

9 798223 850519